The Piano

Millicent Isherwood

Oxford University Press
Music Department, Ely House,
37 Dover Street, London W1X 4AH

Oxford Topics in Music

Edited by Kenneth and Valerie McLeish

Pop Music
Indian Music
The Steel Band
The Piano
Medieval Music
Jamaican Music

In preparation
Opera
The Guitar
Jazz

Designed by Jean Whitcombe
Illustrated by Brian Ainsworth and Roger Gorringe

About the series
These short, illustrated information books are designed to
explore a range of musical topics of interest to 11–14 year olds.
Since reading and fact-gathering should never be a substitute
for listening to or playing music a number of suggestions for
practical work are included, though in some cases these may be
only the starting point for the musical work that could be related
to a particular topic. The books can be used in a variety of ways:
for example, three together might form the core for class, group
or individual work, For older children, the books would be a
useful source of reference for examination projects.

The painting reproduced on the inside front cover is by the German
artist Zoffany, and shows an 18th-century English family making
music, with the lady playing a square piano.

ACKNOWLEDGEMENTS

PHOTOGRAPHS
Page 5 National Gallery; p. 6 Victoria and Albert Museum (2); p. 7
(left) National Gallery, (right) British Museum; p. 8 Cooper-Bridgeman
Library (by kind permission of Viscount de L'Isle); P. 11 (left)
Smithsonian Library, (right) Broadwood and Sons; P. 12 Broadwood
and Sons; p. 15 Metropolitan Museum, New York; p. 16
Beethoven-Haus, Bonn; p. 17 Archiv für Kunst und Geschichte, Berlin;
p. 18 Steinway and Sons; p. 19 Mary Evans Picture Library; p. 20
Royal College of Music; p. 21 British Museum (2); p. 22 (left) Mary
Evans Picture Library, (right) British Museum; p. 24 (top) Mansell
Collection, (bottom) Archiv für Kunst und Geschichte; p. 25 Punch;
p. 27 Bibliothèque Nationale; p. 28 (left) BBC Open University (2),
(top right) Goethehaus, Frankfurt (2), (bottom right) Robert Morley
and Co.; p. 29 Hulton Picture Library; p. 30 J. Butler Kearney; p. 31
(left) J. Butler Kearney, (right) Mansell Collection; p. 32 (left) N. K.
Howarth, (right) Mansell Collection; p. 34 Mary Evans Picture Library;
p. 35 British Museum; p. 36 British Museum; p. 38 University of
London Music Library (2); p. 40 (top left) Mansell Collection, (top
right) British Museum, (bottom) National Gallery, Berlin; p. 41 British
Library; p. 43 David Redfern; p. 44 Novosti Press Agency; p. 46
Performing Arts Services; p. 47 (left) Performing Arts Services, (right)
Novosti Press Agency; p. 48 David Redfern (3).

Inside front cover Yale Center for British Art (Paul Mellon Collection)
Inside back cover Max Jones

© Millicent Isherwood 1981

First published 1981
Second impression 1983
ISBN 0 19 321331 1

Filmset and printed in Great Britain by
BAS Printers Limited, Over Wallop, Hampshire

Contents

Introduction

The piano is one of the most popular of all musical instruments. Its main appeal is its *completeness*: on a piano, you can make all the sounds you need, without needing an accompanist (as violins or flutes do, for example). Many people believe that the piano is mechanically and musically the finest of all keyboard instruments (where you make the sound not by blowing and bowing, but by pressing down a key). Certainly some of the finest classical music has been written for pianists to play.

This book begins with a short account of keyboard instruments before the piano: harpsichord, spinet and the others. (Most are still used today, though the piano has replaced them in popularity.) Then we go on to the workings of the piano. Next come chapters on its history: makers, teachers, home performers, and virtuoso players. The last two chapters are about piano music, its composers and performers of today.

For a young musician, the piano is an ideal instrument to learn. If you play already, we hope this book gives you extra pleasure. If you don't, we hope its glimpse into the fascination of the piano will whet your appetite to learn.

A painting, by a Dutch artist, of a young woman seated at the ▶ virginals. The instrument in the foreground is a viol.

1 Before the piano...

Early keyboard instruments

One of the earliest kinds of keyboard instrument was the **clavichord**, known in Europe from the 15th century onwards. It was the smallest, softest sounding and most delicate. Pressing down the clavichord keys caused small pieces of metal (called 'tangents') to strike the strings. As the tangent stayed on the string, the sound made was very soft, which was just right for a house but no use in a church or concert-hall.

Three other early keyboard instruments were the **harpsichord, virginals** and **spinet**. All three of them make the strings sound in the same way. The strings are *plucked* by a quill or a piece of hard leather which is fixed into a wooden rod, called a jack. The jack is about 12·5 cm to 20 cm high and sits at right-angles to the key. As the key goes down, the jack pops up and its quill plucks the string as it is pushed up past it.

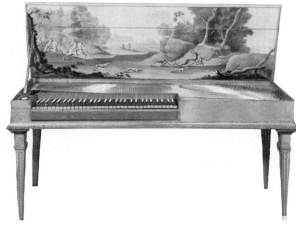

▲ A clavichord made in Germany in 1751

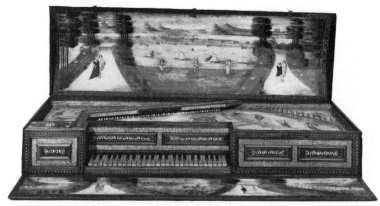

▲ Virginals made by the Englishman Thomas White in 1642

Virginals and spinets had one small keyboard, one string to each key, and one jack to each string. The Latin word for rod or jack was 'virga', so the instrument was called a *virginals*. An Elizabethan with a sense of humour said the instrument had this name because it was played by virgins. Some people believed him, but we know the Elizabethans used many Latin words and all schools then taught Latin. The spinet may have been so-called because its name comes from the French *épinette* (*épine* = a thorn). Perhaps this referred to the thorn-like shape of the jack.

The harpsichord

The harpsichord was also known as a **clavicembalo** or **cembalo** (pronounced 'chembalo'). It is the biggest, grandest, and most complicated of all early keyboard instruments. It has two keyboards and as many as seven pedals. Each pedal moves a whole row of jacks (each row differently made, placed, and shaped) to give different kinds of sound, some loud, others soft. One set of jacks makes the harpsichord sound like a lute (an early, beautiful instrument rather like a guitar) and the pedal that works these jacks is called a 'lute stop'.

▲ The young woman playing a harpsichord. The boy in the doorway is holding an instrument called a theorbo.

The two keyboards could be mechanically 'coupled' so that playing a note on one keyboard caused another (an octave away) on the other keyboard to sound as well. Players did not change pedals too often because you could hear a clicking as the new row of jacks came into play. The harpsichord has a brilliant sound, though each sound dies away fairly soon.

The continuo

By the end of the 16th century (around 1600), the harpsichord was loud enough to play with the orchestra in the opera-houses and concert-halls and it kept everything together. The harpsichordist played a written bass part with his left hand. On top he played harmonies, and filled in for missing instruments. He also set the speed and gave the signal to begin. In other words, he took on the role of conductor. This harpsichord part was called the **continuo** as it was 'on the go' continuously all through the piece. The composer usually played this important part, directing his own music from the harpsichord. Bach and Handel often played continuo in performances of their own music.

▲ A 17th-century concert ticket designed by the famous artist Hogarth. The harpsichordist on the right is providing the continuo.

7

Music for the virginals and harpsichord

Music for the virginals was popular in Elizabeth I's time. The Queen played very well and encouraged composers, among them **William Byrd**, **Giles Farnaby**, **Dr. John Bull**, and **Thomas Morley**, by rewarding them. These men were successful then and are famous now for their virginals music.

They wrote dance music (the Queen loved dancing) such as jigs, pavans, galliards, lavoltas, and bransles (pronounced 'brawls'). They wrote song-tunes with variations, using popular songs of the day. Compositions were written down by hand and some famous manuscript (handwritten) books are *My Ladye Nevell's Booke of Virginal Music* by William Byrd; *Benjamin Cosyn's Virginal Book* (Cosyn copied pieces by Byrd, Bull, and Gibbons as well as some of his own compositions); *The Fitzwilliam Virginal Book* (kept in the Fitzwilliam Museum in Cambridge). The first *printed* virginals music in England was called *Parthenia* and appeared in 1612.

Much Elizabethan keyboard music was descriptive, such as 'The Battell', 'The Primerose', 'The Fall of the Leaf', 'His Grief', 'His Toy', 'His Rest', 'The King's Hunt'.

Famous composers of keyboard music in other countries included Frescobaldi in Italy (1583–1643), and Cabezon in Spain (1510–1566). Froberger from Germany (1616–1667) studied with Frescobaldi and visited England.

Music for the harpsichord was written by **François Couperin** (1668–1733) in France; **Domenico Scarlatti** (1685–1757) who was Italian but went to work in Spain; **George Frideric Handel** (1685–1759) who was German but came to live in England; and **J. S. Bach** (1685–1750) who lived and worked in Germany.

▲ Queen Elizabeth I dancing with Lord Dudley

Questions

1 Name four types of early keyboard instrument.
2 How did the virginals and spinet get their names?
3 In which ways was the harpsichord different from the virginals and spinet?
4 Name three famous manuscripts of early keyboard music.
5 What types of keyboard music were written in Elizabeth I's time?
6 Describe the job of the harpsichordist in an early 18th-century orchestra.

Projects

1 Find out all you can about the composers for the virginals and the harpsichord.
2 Try to visit a museum which has some old keyboard instruments. Draw and describe some of those you see.

2 How it began and how it works

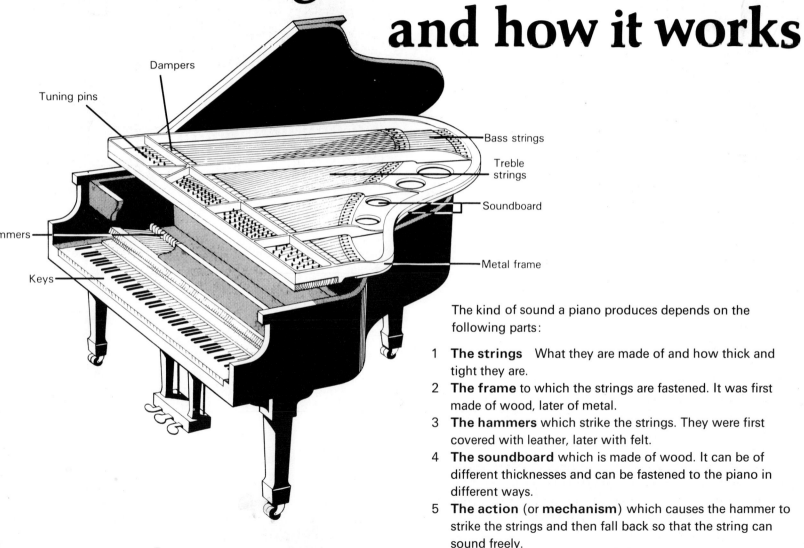

Dampers

Tuning pins

Bass strings

Treble strings

Soundboard

Hammers

Metal frame

Keys

The kind of sound a piano produces depends on the following parts:

1 **The strings**   What they are made of and how thick and tight they are.
2 **The frame** to which the strings are fastened. It was first made of wood, later of metal.
3 **The hammers** which strike the strings. They were first covered with leather, later with felt.
4 **The soundboard** which is made of wood. It can be of different thicknesses and can be fastened to the piano in different ways.
5 **The action** (or **mechanism**) which causes the hammer to strike the strings and then fall back so that the string can sound freely.

The first piano

Earlier keyboard instruments (virginals, harpsichord, and clavichord) used strings, keys, and a soundboard, but made the same strength of sound however you pressed the key down. But the piano was different. Its action (that is, the mechanism used to make the strings sound) enabled sound to be made *loud* by pressing the key down forcibly, and *soft* by pressing the key down gently. That is why the *piano* was originally called *fortepiano* and *pianoforte*. All three names are Italian because the first piano was made in Italy. *Piano* is Italian for 'soft' and *forte* means 'loud' or 'strong'. These words were used to describe the first keyboard instrument which could make the same string sound both soft and loud.

The strings

These vibrate to make sound. (*Vibrate* means tremble or shake.) The sound made will be *high-pitched* if the string is short or thin and very tightly-stretched; and it will be *low-pitched* if the

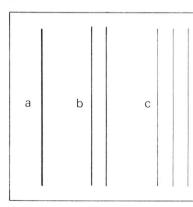

Stringing on the modern piano. Each of the instrument's bass notes has only one string (a), whereas middle notes each have two finer strings (b), and top notes three still finer ones (c). All piano strings are made of steel, but bass strings are copper-wound to increase the resonance.

1750 - most had 5 octaves   c' is middle C

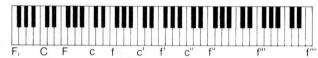

1809 - most had 6 octaves

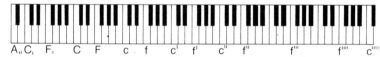

Modern piano

The extending of the piano's range from its beginning until today.

string is long or thick and less tightly-stretched. You will be able to sing at the same pitch as the sound made by the notes in the middle of the piano. The notes made by the strings on the *right* of the piano will be *higher in pitch* than you can sing. The strings on the left as you face the keyboard will sound *lower in pitch* than you can sing.

At first, **steel** was used for the treble (that is, the higher-pitched) strings, and **brass** for the bass (that is, the lower-pitched) strings. Then steel was used for all the strings, but the lower strings were **wrapped**. That means that an extra covering was wound round and round the string from top to bottom to make it thick. The thickness of the strings ranges from 0·70 to 1·50 millimetres.

To make the strings give a full (resonant) sound there are two or even three strings of the same length and thickness to every key, that is, to every note. So many strings are used that makers finally had the idea of cross-stringing and over-stringing. The pictures opposite will show you at once what those words mean.

The frame

The strings have to be stretched tight to give each string the correct pitch, to make all the Gs (and all the other notes) match as they should. This puts an enormous strain on the frame. The early pianos had wooden frames, which collapsed if the strings were stretched too tight. Therefore the piano needed tuning very often (even as often as twice during a concert). When the metal frame came into use, more strings could be used for each note and pianos were given extra notes at the top and bottom. They had five octaves at first but by 1824 they had seven.

▲ Over-stringing on a Steinway square piano of 1878

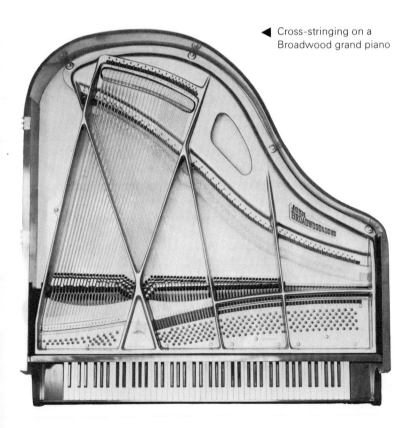

◀ Cross-stringing on a Broadwood grand piano

The hammers

These were made of wood but the hammer head was covered to improve the quality of sound. Many kinds of cover were tried, including cork, sponge, flannel, sheepskin, buckskin. Leather was the most popular covering until Henri Pape of Paris used felt. His felt covering for hammers was his most important invention, although altogether he patented 137.

The soundboard

This *amplifies* the sound made by the strings (that means it makes the sound louder and fuller). It is made of wood and is to be found under the strings of the grand piano and at the back of the upright piano. In both cases it is attached to the metal frame. It acts as an amplifier for the sound-waves from the strings. The wood was carefully chosen and seasoned. Mozart wrote to his father in 1777 describing how the piano-maker Stein left the wood outside for months in rain, snow, wind, and sun so that it would crack. Then Stein would seal up the cracks and know that it would not crack any more as it grew older.

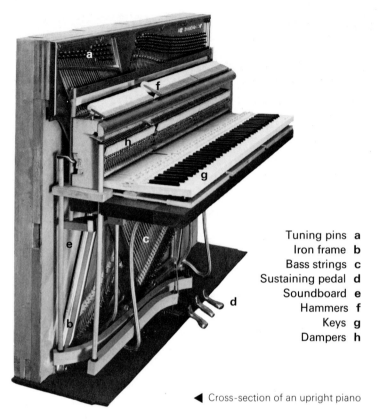

Tuning pins **a**
Iron frame **b**
Bass strings **c**
Sustaining pedal **d**
Soundboard **e**
Hammers **f**
Keys **g**
Dampers **h**

◀ Cross-section of an upright piano

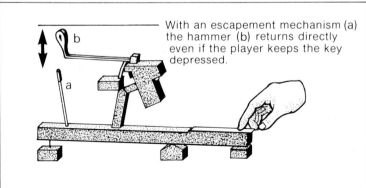

With an escapement mechanism (a) the hammer (b) returns directly even if the player keeps the key depressed.

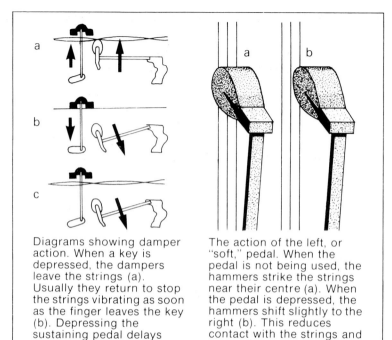

Diagrams showing damper action. When a key is depressed, the dampers leave the strings (a). Usually they return to stop the strings vibrating as soon as the finger leaves the key (b). Depressing the sustaining pedal delays damper action on all strings until the foot is raised (c).

The action of the left, or "soft," pedal. When the pedal is not being used, the hammers strike the strings near their centre (a). When the pedal is depressed, the hammers shift slightly to the right (b). This reduces contact with the strings and so produces a softer tone.

The action

When the key is pressed down, the hammer hits the string and makes it vibrate. If the hammer rested on the string, the string couldn't vibrate properly. So the hammer has to bounce *back* again when it has hit the string. The early pianos had a simple action where a 'mopstick' knocked the hammer up on to the string and then it fell back. The trouble was that the hammer sometimes bounced too energetically and hit the string a second time on the rebound. To prevent this, an 'escapement' was invented which caught the hammer so it couldn't bounce back. It wasn't easy then to repeat the same note quickly. So a 'double escapement' was invented.

It is important to stop or **damp** the sound so that the notes do not run into each other and sound together when they do not harmonize (or mix well together). So each string has a **damper**, a soft pad which stops the sound when the player releases the key.

But sometimes a composer *wants* the sounds to mingle with each other and plans this effect. Then *all* the dampers must be held off the strings. This is done by the **right pedal**. It is called the **sustaining pedal** because it sustains (or holds on) the sounds by lifting off *all* the dampers so the notes go on sounding.

The **left pedal** is used less often than the right pedal. It is used in piano music when the composer wants a soft, mysterious sound.

On a grand piano, the left pedal moves the action a little to one side, so that the hammers strike only one string for each note instead of all the strings for that note. Upright pianos work differently. Sometimes the left pedal moves the hammers nearer to the strings so they don't hit the strings so hard. In some upright pianos, a piece of material is moved between the hammers and the strings so that the sound is softened, or **muted**.

Questions

1 What do the words *piano* and *forte* mean?
2 Name the five parts of the piano that cause it to sound.
3 Does a thin, short string make a high or low sound? What kind of sound does a thick, long string make?
4 How did Stein season his soundboards?
5 What is used to cover the hammer-heads in modern pianos?

Projects

Before you read on please note something very important. **Pianos are very heavy. They are dangerous if they fall. Never move a piano or take off the front panel unless there is an adult with you.**

1 Get a dulcimer, glockenspiel, chime-bar, cymbal, or triangle. Strike it with a beater or drumstick. Let the beater stay on it and the sound will be dull. Let the beater bounce off and the sound will be bright. Let the sound ring on, then touch the instrument with your hand and you will stop the sound, that is, you will 'damp' it.
2 **Ask an adult** to remove the front of the piano so you can see the action. Look for the strings, the hammers, the dampers.
    a Gently press down a key. Watch what happens.
    b Press down the right pedal. What happens?
    c Press down the left pedal. What happens?
    d Ask someone who can play a piece of music to do so. Watch what happens.
3 (Take this slowly, one step at a time.) Very slowly press down a G and B in the middle of the piano. Do this slowly so that the notes *do not sound*. Hold them down carefully. Now get someone else to play very strongly and sharply two very low Gs, which should *not* be held down. The notes that you are holding down, the G and B in the middle, will then give out a 'ghost' sound. This sound is called **sympathetic vibration**. Can you guess why? If you read through the part about dampers and the right pedal on this page you might be able to work it out.

3 Famous piano-makers and the spread of the piano

1709	Cristofori made one of the first pianos in Italy.
1733	Silbermann made a piano in Germany. (The King of Prussia had fifteen Silbermann pianos by 1747.)
1760	Zumpe left Germany to make and sell pianos in England.
1766	John Burton of Yorkshire composed and published *Ten Sonatas for the Pianoforte* – some of the first actual 'piano' music ever written.
1767	A piano was used to accompany a singer at a London Concert.
1768	The first public piano concert. J. C. Bach played on a Zumpe piano which had cost him £50.
1774	A piano was made in Philadelphia, U.S.A., by John Brent.
1777	Broadwood made pianos in England, Érard in France, and Stein in Augsburg. (Broadwood made 400 a year by 1800.)
1783	Broadwood invented the sustaining pedal. (See page 13.)
1795	In England the piano replaced the harpsichord in the King's Band.
1816	Broadwoods sent a piano to Beethoven, who wrote the 'Hammerklavier' sonata.
1820	The English patented the first all-metal frame.
1822	Érard invented the 'double escapement' action.
1840	Pianos made with a full range of seven octaves.
1851	The Great Exhibition in London was opened by Queen Victoria. It was one of many Trade Fairs in Europe and America. Many pianos were shown, and bought.

Italy

Bartolomeo Cristofori was born in Italy in 1655. He became a maker of harpsichords in Padua. Then he was employed by Prince Ferdinand de' Medici in Florence. Cristofori worked for him in Florence as maker, keeper, and repairer of musical instruments. He made a piano around 1709. Cristofori called his invention a 'clavicembalo col piano e forte' (a harpsichord with soft and loud).

Descriptions of the new instrument were printed in a scientific journal in Venice in 1711 and in Germany in 1725. Cristofori went on to make bigger and better pianos. His new instrument was thought to be exactly right for accompanying singers and

◀ A piano made by
Bartolomeo Cristofori

other instruments, for playing solos and playing with orchestras, but it was thought to have too small a sound to be used in church.

Cristofori invented the effect you get when you press down the left pedal of a grand piano today (see page 13). He used knobs at the side to alter the position of the keyboard. He died in 1731. Only two of his pianos still exist. Here is a picture of one of them.

Germany

In Germany, people read accounts of Cristofori's piano. One of these people was **Gottfried Silbermann**, born in Saxony in 1683. He was a famous organ-builder as well as maker of harpsichords and pianos. There are some funny stories about him. As a boy in the village where he was born, he tricked some simple people into digging for buried treasure in a ruined building at night. Then he fired off guns to frighten them. Once he was building an organ in a convent (which takes a long time) and he persuaded a nun to elope with him. They were caught as they set off. If he wasn't satisfied with the tone of an instrument when he had built it, he destroyed it with an axe. Once he built an organ and when he played it there was a rattle in the church. He couldn't find where the rattle came from, but thinking it might be one of the windows he smashed the window. (Perhaps these stories were untrue, but they were probably good for advertisement.)

Silbermann read about Cristofori's piano and made one himself. He showed it to the famous organist, teacher, and composer Johann Sebastian Bach in 1730. Bach didn't much like it, saying the sound was weak in the treble (where the higher notes are) and that the action was stiff (that is, heavy and hard to play). Silbermann was angry at first but later he tried again and improved his pianos. The King of Prussia, Frederick the Great, liked Silbermann's pianos and bought 15 of them.

Frederick employed many musicians, including J. S. Bach's son, Carl Philipp Emanuel Bach. In 1747 the King invited old J. S. Bach to his court. Bach played a Silbermann piano and said he liked it. Perhaps he did. Perhaps he was just being polite to the King. Anyway, he never owned one himself.

Stein

Silbermann had apprentices who learned how to build pianos. **Andreas Stein** was one. He began making pianos in Augsburg and his pianos were so good that he sold them to people who lived many miles from Augsburg. He played the piano, and so did his daughter Nanette, who was a child prodigy (that means that she played extraordinarily well at an early age). When the composer Mozart visited the Steins he heard Nanette play and although he said she had 'genius' he also said she had been badly taught. She pulled faces and rolled her eyes when she played, and made Mozart want to laugh. Her hands and arms moved more than they needed to and she missed some notes out when she played fast pieces. She grew up to be a famous pianist, a singer, and a writer of books. She married a piano-maker called **Streicher** who made pianos in Vienna. We described on page 11 how much trouble her father Andreas Stein took to season his soundboards. Some of them are still in perfect condition now, even though they are 200 years old.

Stein moved to Vienna and his pianos were so good that **Haydn**, **Mozart**, and **Beethoven** all began to prefer the piano to the harpsichord. Stein pianos had a clear tone and were excellent for playing rapid passages. Stein also studied hearing and deafness. He was a friend of Beethoven, and after Beethoven went deaf Stein supplied him with various kinds of ear-trumpet to try to help him to hear.

The piano moves to England

Zumpe

Another apprentice of Silbermann was **Johannes Zumpe**. The Seven Years War lasted from 1756 to 1763 in Germany and Zumpe decided to move to England where he could make and sell pianos. He made the 'square' piano (which is really oblong). These pianos were instantly popular. They were small, the action was simple, and they were easy to carry. Zumpe delivered them carrying the main part on his back and holding the legs in his arms. As they were easier to make than the bigger 'grand' pianos they were also cheaper to buy. Dr. Charles Burney wrote in his *History of Music* that there was 'scarcely a house in the kingdom' that had ever had a keyboard instrument that did not now buy a Zumpe 'square' piano. Zumpe could hardly make them fast enough and soon had to stop delivering them himself. They had a very sweet, pleasant tone. The map on page 14 shows Zumpe exporting square pianos to England. And there is a picture of a square piano by Broadwood, on page 28.

The Zumpe piano was first heard in public in England in 1767. During the interval of a popular theatre-piece called *The Beggar's Opera* it was used by Mr. Dibdin to accompany the singing of Miss Brickler. A year later, a Zumpe piano was used

▲ Beethoven's ear trumpets, made for him by the piano-maker Stein

Broadwood

John Broadwood of London introduced many new ideas into piano-making. He improved the dampers and invented the right pedal (see page 13). He invented a new hammer-action, and a new way of stringing so that the bass gave a clearer, richer sound. By 1794 his pianos had a range of six octaves. Broadwood made a piano for Beethoven who was delighted with it, and the firm made a piano specially for Chopin when he came to give concerts in England. This firm still makes pianos and is the oldest piano-making firm in the world.

France

Sebastien Érard was born in Strasbourg in 1752. By the time he was 16, he was apprenticed to a harpsichord-maker in Paris. He made such beautiful harpsichords that a Duchess gave him living quarters and a workshop in her château (French for 'castle'). Here he made his first pianoforte. Érard played his new instrument to all the Duchess's friends and relations. He got so many orders that he brought his brother to Paris and set up a workshop there.

Dealers who had been importing English Zumpe and Broadwood pianos got so angry at Érard's success that they raided his shop. They said Érard was breaking the law (in making pianos) because he was not in the right Guild (or Trade Union). Érard appealed to the French King, Louis XVI, who gave him a special licence. The importers of English pianos were right to worry, because imports fell after Érard's pianos were available. They were like Zumpe's pianos at first, but then Érard invented the 'double escapement', which has been used ever since (see page 12).

When the French Revolution broke out and Louis XVI was beheaded, Érard came to London and opened a works and a

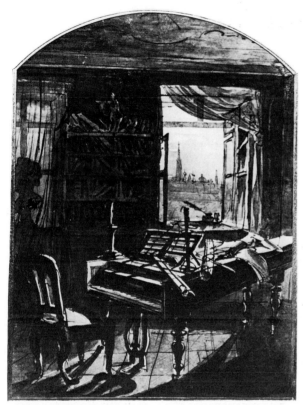
▲ Beethoven's study in Vienna

in the first public piano concert ever given anywhere. The performer at this concert was Johann Christian Bach, the youngest son of J. S. Bach and brother of Carl Philipp Emmanuel. He came to live in London and became known as 'the London Bach'. Zumpe's pianos were popular in France too.

English pianos became very famous on the continent. Their action was different from the Viennese piano-action. The tone was warmer, thicker, richer, and more resonant. But the keys of the Viennese pianos were lighter and easier to press down, so it was easier to play more rapidly on them than on English ones.

shop there, leaving his brother in Paris. He realized how different the English pianos were from those made in France and Germany, so he modified his own pianos. He also invented the **agraffe** — a small metal plate with three holes in it, through which the strings pass. It helps the strings to keep in tune and is still used.

America

The most famous piano-maker who settled in America (and whose firm is still working) was born in Germany. **Heinrich Steinweg** won a medal at the Battle of Waterloo for blowing his bugle in the face of the enemy. He married, had ten children, and became a piano-maker. In 1848 there was war in Europe so

Portrait of the piano-maker Henry Steinway ▶

the family emigrated to New York. Heinrich Steinweg changed his name to **Henry Steinway**. His sons studied science, engineering, music, and acoustics. In 1854 the Steinway piano won prizes at the Washington and New York Trade Fairs. The woods used in making one piano, to get the best effects, included mahogany, walnut, spruce, poplar, maple, sugar-pine, and rosewood. Steinway compiled huge volumes of research-notes and pioneered many new methods. This firm of piano-makers is probably the most famous in the world today.

Questions

1   What did people think of Cristofori's new instrument?
2   What was the first occasion that a Zumpe piano was heard in England?
3   Which piano had the heavier action, the English or the Viennese? Which played longer-lasting sounds? On which could you play fast notes more easily?
4   What improvements did John Broadwood make to the piano?
5   What happened when Érard set up his workshop in Paris?
6   What woods were used in making just one Steinway piano?

Projects

Conduct a **survey**. Choose a number of people — the pupils in one class, or a group of people who live in your street. Ask them these questions and compare the answers.

a   Have you a piano?
b   Is it a grand piano or an upright?
c   What make is it?
d   How many octaves has it?
e   Have you a record-player?
f   How many records have you?
g   How many of the records are piano records?

Teachers and pupils

As more and more piano-makers set up workshops and prospered, the piano invaded 'every respectable home' in Europe. Piano teachers also prospered. One English girls' school advertised — 'Lessons from a master one guinea (£1.05p); lessons from a mistress 5/- (25p)'. By 1779 there were said to be 300 piano teachers in Vienna.

There was (and still is) a great deal of argument about the 'right' way to play a piano. Some players make pianos sound better than others. Some treat pianos very harshly. The piano needs more tuning and repair if it is not carefully and well played. 'Gentleness achieves more than violence' is the golden rule. But there is more to it than that.

C.P.E.Bach

The first book about how to play was written by J. S. Bach's second son, **Carl Philipp Emanuel Bach** (1714–1788) (see page 16). It was intitled *An Essay on the True Art of Playing Keyboard Instruments.* It was very long. Part One was published in 1753, Part Two in 1762. Haydn, Mozart, and Beethoven used the book and recommended it to their pupils. C. P. E. Bach was keyboard-player to King Frederick the Great of Prussia for nearly thirty years. His job became boring as the King insisted on playing the flute nearly every evening, and not always well. Bach had to accompany the King and the other court musicians in flute concertos and other pieces.

Dr. Charles Burney, the English scholar who wrote a *History of Music* (see page 16) and other books about music, visited C. P. E. Bach while touring Europe. Dr Burney thought that this Bach was the most expressive player he had ever heard.

J.C.Bach's Subscription Concerts

Dr. Burney had heard C. P. E. Bach's younger brother play in England, and greatly admired him, too. **Johann Christian Bach** (1735–1782) left Germany when the Seven Years War began. He worked in Italy and then came to England. He lodged in London with an old pupil of his father's called Carl Abel. Together they gave many concerts in London, in Vauxhall Gardens and in the Hanover Square Rooms.

These concerts were called 'Subscription Concerts' as people

◀ Carl Philipp Emanuel Bach, Bach's third son

▲ Johann Christian Bach. Portrait by the English painter Gainsborough

▲ An 18th-century concert in the Vauxhall Gardens, London

were asked to subscribe to (that is, to buy tickets for) a series, or set of concerts. It was at one of these concerts that J. C. Bach gave the first-ever piano recital. The series of concerts was so popular that in one year J. C. Bach made a profit of over £3,000. That year the rent for his house (for the whole year) was only £30 and meat was 5p a pound. This shows how successful he was. The Queen appointed him as her piano-teacher. He was so well known that he attracted a large number of piano-pupils. Being the Queen's teacher helped, but he was famous in any case for being a good teacher.

He wrote a lot of pleasant music for his young pupils to play as they were learning. His difficult music he played himself at his concerts.

In 1764 the eight-year-old Mozart visited London to give concerts. He was already a brilliant performer on the keyboard. J. C. Bach gave him help and advice. Mozart never forgot him and wrote to his father years later:

'I love him, as you know, and respect him with all my heart.'

Mozart himself only taught pupils when he was very hard up (which unhappily was quite often). He hated teaching and complained about it in his letters home.

21

Beethoven and Czerny

Ludwig van Beethoven (1770–1827) only taught very talented pupils. He taught the twelve-year-old **Carl Czerny** (1791–1857) for two years. Czerny later talked a lot about Beethoven's method of teaching, because he was proud to have been the pupil of the greatest composer who ever lived.

Beethoven, the teacher . . . ▶

◀ and Carl Czerny, one of his pupils

Beethoven was so deaf by the time Czerny went to him that the lessons must have been difficult for both of them. Beethoven gave Czerny lots of scales and exercises to practise and told him to read C. P. E. Bach's book (page 20). Just before Beethoven died he told a friend he had wanted to write a book on how to play the piano. Beethoven had been a great virtuoso pianist before he went deaf, but he had to stop playing in public when he could no longer hear how loud or soft he was playing.

Czerny himself became a famous teacher who wrote an enormous amount of music for his pupils. Some of it was for beginners and some was very difficult. He wrote 861 books of piano pieces and very few people learn the piano today without playing some of his pieces. His most famous pupil was **Franz Liszt**.

Clementi and Hummel

Muzio Clementi (1752–1832) played pianos, taught pupils to play, composed and published piano music, made pianos and sold them in England, Europe, and Russia. He was born in Rome. His father was a poor man. An Englishman, the Honourable Peter Beckford, met the fourteen-year-old Clementi in Rome, recognized his musical talent, and, in Beckford's own words, 'bought him from his father for seven years'. So Clementi travelled to Dorset where the wealthy Mr. Beckford had a large mansion. Here he studied and practised the piano until he was 21.

In 1773 Clementi gave concerts in London and was tremendously successful. He published music which was different from any written before. It made the most of the

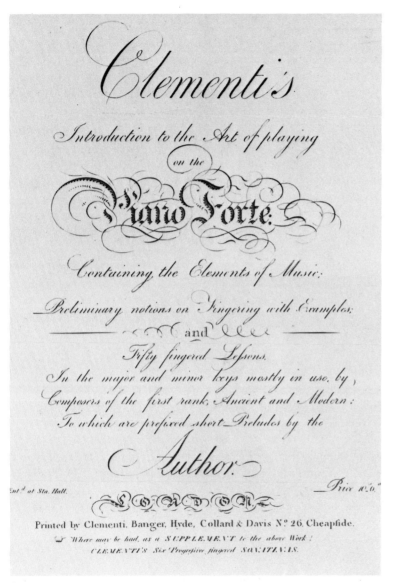

▲ The title page from Clementi's *Introduction to the Art of playing on the Pianoforte*

piano's special qualities — **legato** playing (smooth playing where each note is joined to its neighbouring note), **staccato** (each note played spikily, sharply, separate from its neighbouring notes), **crescendo** (pronounced 'creshendo' and meaning 'gradually getting louder'), **diminuendo** (gradually getting softer), and **cantabile** (pronounced 'kantarbilay' and meaning 'in a singing tone')

In 1800, Clementi wrote a book about how to play, called *An Introduction to the Art of playing on the Pianoforte.* He charged more money for lessons than anyone ever had before. He made pupils pay in advance. He wrote good, easy music for young pupils.

In 1817, Clementi published a book of 'studies' which progressed from very easy to more difficult as one played through the book. Each study gave practice in some technical difficulty—playing fast runs, fast chords, playing 'singing tunes' with soft, quick accompaniments. The book had a Latin title, *Gradus ad Parnassum.* This means 'One step at a time to the top of the mountain' (Parnassus was a mountain in ancient Greece dedicated to Apollo, the god of music). Beethoven, Chopin and Brahms used Clementi's studies and taught them to their pupils. Clementi retired a rich man and bought a country estate at Evesham. When he died he was buried in Westminster Abbey.

In 1827 a book with a long title was published – *A Complete Theoretical and Practical Course of Instruction in the Art of Playing the Pianoforte, commencing with the Simplest Elementary Principles, and including every information requisite to the Most Finished Style of Performance.* This was by **Johann Hummel** (1778–1837), one of the few pupils Mozart enjoyed teaching. Hummel visited London and gave a concert in the Hanover Square Rooms when he was 14 years old. He had lessons from Clementi. In 1802 Mozart's widow gave a party. Both Beethoven and Czerny (aged 11) were there and heard

Hummel play. Czerny was thrilled to hear such splendid playing, but surprised by Hummel's appearance. He expected a famous pianist to be well-dressed and good-looking, but Hummel was badly dressed, not very clean, wore several diamond rings, and had a twitchy face badly scarred by smallpox.

In Vienna people compared Beethoven and Hummel as pianists. Beethoven's playing was fiery, noisy, with tremendous character and strength. Hummel's playing was distinct, delicate, elegant, and charming. But whereas Beethoven never wrote his book on how to play the piano, Hummel's book was read by all serious pianists for many years after his death. It survived longer than the music he wrote, which is not much played now. He wrote a lot of dance music and variations on popular songs of the day.

Portrait of Chopin by the ▶
French painter Delacroix

Chopin and Liszt

Chopin's pupils were mostly wealthy Parisians. Although Chopin was a specially gifted composer and performer, he had new ideas about playing and teaching the piano. There had been a persistent idea that the thumbs should never play black notes. Chopin wrote music that made this necessary. He wrote studies that were more than just exercises, but were tuneful and exciting pieces as well.

Liszt had an enormous number of pupils because he gave public lessons. 40 or 50 pupils would come and put their music on the piano. After a long wait, the master, Liszt, would appear. He looked through the pile of music, chose a piece, and the pupil who had put it there came forward to play in front of all the others, who listened to the lesson. Then another pupil was chosen in the same way. So some of Liszt's pupils never got to play to him at all.

◀ Portrait of Liszt,
aged 36, in 1847

Tobias Matthay

Tobias Matthay (1858–1946) created a method which combined his own successful techniques with those of great teachers of the past. He analysed what happened to the muscles of hand, arm, shoulder, and fingers when playing. He also analysed what happened inside the instrument itself. He then tried to sweep away all the old rules that didn't seem necessary or helpful. He wrote books about his method but they were hard to understand. He would say 'Go to my pupils and they will show you what I mean'. He had extremely successful pupils, like Dame Myra Hess, who were noted for their beautiful tone and the rich sound they coaxed from pianos. Professor Harold Craxton (a pupil of Matthay's) would say to his own pupils 'You know, if we were selling this piano, I'd get a better price for it than you would'. He always made the piano sound with a richer, sweeter tone than the pupil did.

Different teaching methods

You will have noticed that all the famous teachers mentioned so far were themselves playing in public at an early age. But a good teacher does not necessarily have to be a famous performer. There is no single 'best' teaching method. Everything depends on how sensitive an ear the player has. Teachers help their pupils' ears to be knowledgeable and critical.

Position of the stool

Some teachers said the stood should be on the left to help the hands with the heavy bass strings. Others said the stool should be on the right to help the hands make the weaker treble strings sound stronger. Clementi and Mozart put it in the centre of the keyboard. Later, when the piano became seven octaves wide, it had to be always in the centre or the player could not reach both ends. Some players used high stools, some preferred low ones.

Position of the hands

Some teachers said the hands ought to be close to the keys, others played with hands flying high above the keys. Clementi made pupils play with coins on the backs of their hands. If the coin stayed on, the pupil could keep it. Some teachers made their pupils play dreary 'five-finger exercises' for 20 or 30 minutes every day. This was supposed to make all fingers equally strong. But, as Chopin said, this was 'flying in the face of nature' as all fingers don't have the same tendons and muscles. There is an exercise on page 26 which shows this.

Some teachers said that the hand should turn so that the thumb was well over the keys. Some said that the hand should turn so that the little finger was well over the keys. Some liked the elbows out. Others liked them tucked neatly in to the side of the body.

Fingering

There were many rules about fingering. It is true that fingering is vitally important when playing advanced music. Good habits have to be formed early. But hard and fast rules don't allow for the endless variety of notes that a composer can use when writing for the piano.

Practising

Chopin thought three hours a day was long enough to practise as the mind could not pay attention longer than that. Many pianists were trained to do eight hours' practice daily.

Questions

1 Who wrote *An Essay on the True Art of Playing Keyboard Instruments*?
2 Who was piano-teacher to the Queen of England?
3 Who were pupils of (*a*) Beethoven, (*b*) Mozart, (*c*) Czerny, (*d*) Clementi?
4 What was the title of the book Hummel wrote?
5 What do these Italian words mean: (*a*) *piano*, (*b*) *forte*, (*c*) *crescendo*, (*d*) *diminuendo*, (*e*) *cantabile*?
6 What is the name of Clementi's book of studies? What does it mean?

Projects

1 Sit in front of the centre of the keyboard (see page 10). Let your right hand play F, then A, then C with thumb, middle finger and little finger. Let left hand play F, then A, then C with little finger, middle finger and thumb. (Right hand will be comfortable on the F A C above middle C and left hand on the F A C below middle C.) When you can do this, move the stool to the right and play the same notes again with both hands. Then move the stool to the left and play again. Which is the easiest place for you to be?
2 Play the same notes again sitting on a high stool. (Put a cushion or a folded coat on a stool.) Then play while sitting on a chair. Then play using a piano stool. Which is easiest?
3 Try playing the three notes with a coin on the back of your hand. Does it slip off?
4 Play five notes, G, A, B, C, D, one with each finger. Play them again with the coin on the back of your hand. Does it slip off? If it stays on, see how fast you can play before it does slip off.
5 Sit at a desk or table. Rest your hand on it with fingers curled so that the tip of each finger is on the surface. While keeping all fingers in this position, lift the thumb up and let it fall back on to the table. Then lift the next finger and let it fall back. Then lift the next, and so on until all have had a turn. Which is the weakest finger? Is it the same with both hands? Why do you think this is so?
6 Get records of the same piece played by different pianists. Listen carefully. Can you hear the difference? Which performance do you prefer and why? (Many pianists have recorded the Chopin Studies, Waltzes, and Ballades.)

5 The piano in the home

Different sorts of piano

Between 1709 and 1840, piano-makers were always bringing out new pianos of all shapes and sizes. One of the main problems was that a grand piano was often too big to fit into the drawing-room of an average-sized family house. In 1816 Clementi made an upright grand piano. If you look at the two pictures you will see that when the doors are closed it doesn't seem to be a piano. When the doors are open you can see the strings, and also the music books (to save space). There were also, apart from 'grand' and 'semi-grand' pianos, 'cottage pianos', 'cabinet pianos', 'square pianos' (really rectangular or oblong), 'giraffe pianos', 'elephant pianos', 'pyramid pianos', and even 'lyre pianos'. The last name is the most odd as the lyre was an ancient Greek instrument not at all like a piano.

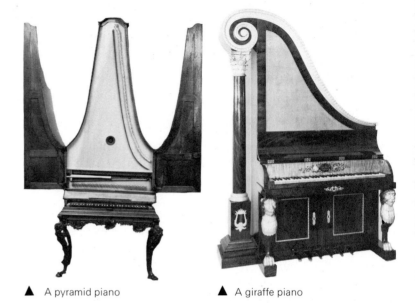

▲ A pyramid piano   ▲ A giraffe piano

Whenever a new model appeared, the wealthy would buy it to add to their collection, while the less wealthy would sell their old one to make way for a new model. James Harrison published a *Pianoforte Magazine* from 1797 to 1802 and anyone who bought all 250 issues got a free piano. (It would have cost 25 guineas (£26.25p) to buy and would have looked like this square piano.)

▲ A Clementi grand piano of 1816, doors closed . . . and open ▲

A Broadwood square piano of 1791 ▶

What was the piano used for?

Two hundred years ago, families spent much more time at home than they do now, because travelling was slow and difficult. In winter roads got so muddy that horses got stuck and could not pull carriages. So people were forced to entertain themselves at home.

The piano was used in the home to play dance-music so that the energetic could dance waltzes, cotillions, and country dances in their drawing rooms and halls. It was used to accompany singers and instrumentalists. The Victorians were very fond of singing ballads, accompanied by piano. It was used for playing piano arrangements of operas, symphonies, and theatre music. For many people, before the days of radio, TV, and record-players, this would be the only way they could hear new music. The wealthy would pay pianists to play to guests in their houses in the evenings, but most people would listen to members of their own families playing as best they could. So piano lessons came to form an important part of people's education, especially for girls.

All young ladies play

In the 18th and 19th centuries marriage was the only way in which a young lady could get a home for herself. If she did not marry she had to live with a relation — her parents, or perhaps a married brother or sister. All girls were taught to expect to marry, to dress and walk and talk attractively, and to be accomplished.

Part of being accomplished was being able to play the piano and sing. Young ladies with little money needed to be very attractive and accomplished to acquire a husband. The writer Maria Edgeworth said:

> 'A young lady is nobody and nothing without accomplishments, they are part of her fortune.'

The novelist William Thackeray wrote:

> 'What causes them to labour at pianoforte sonatas and learn four songs from a fashionable master at a guinea a lesson . . . but the noble ambition of matrimony?'

In Vienna in the 1780s some young ladies even earned their living by playing the piano. Thérèse von Paradis was a blind girl who earned her living by playing, teaching, and composing. Josephine Auernhammer played to Mozart, who thought her a very good pianist. She apparently did not expect to marry (she was very fat, plain, and sweated a lot), but she gave public concerts and was a great success. She did finally marry — perhaps when she had become rich.

Jane Austen and the piano

Jane Austen (who died in 1817) makes fun of the way girls were expected to show off their accomplishments. In her novel *Pride and Prejudice* there is a party and Elizabeth Bennet is asked to play.

'Elizabeth's performance was pleasing, but by no means capital. After a song or two . . . she was eagerly succeeded at the instrument by her sister Mary who was always impatient for display.'

Mary was the plain girl in a family of five sisters and had worked very hard to become accomplished. She knew she played well and so played long, difficult pieces. Her hearers became bored and restless.

'Elizabeth, easy and unaffected, had been listened to with much more pleasure, though not playing half so well', so Mary, after her long piece was ended, was asked to play dance music so that her pretty sisters could dance with the army officers.

In Jane Austen's novel *Emma*, Jane Fairfax plays at a party. Harriet (who is silly) says next day:

'I saw she had execution but if she does play so very well, it is no more than she is obliged to do, because she will have to teach.'

Jane is an army officer's daughter and therefore is a lady. But her father is dead, so she is poor and is to become a governess.

The only way an unmarried young lady could earn her living was as a governess. This meant working long hours for little money. Governesses were expected to teach pupils to read, write, play the piano, and copy music neatly.

▲ Jane Austen's piano in the drawing room of her house in Chawton, Hampshire

At that time (around 1800) people who had made their money in trade were not thought to be 'gentlemen'. They were anxious to make their sons and daughters into gentlemen and ladies. So they bought pianos and their girls learned to play. Jane Austen describes such people (the Coles in *Emma*). As they grow richer, they add to their house and their number of servants, and buy 'a new grandpianoforte', although Mrs. Cole said she 'did not know one note from another, and our little girls, who are but just beginning, perhaps may never make anything of it.'

Ladies of leisure

Some ladies really enjoyed their music, however. Servants were cheap to hire, and music passed the time of the girl who had little housework to do. Jane Austen herself liked music and played the piano every day. Much of the music she played was from manuscript, neatly copied out by herself. This photograph of Jane Austen's manuscript book was taken at her cottage in Chawton in Hampshire, which you may visit. One of the tunes she copied was the *Marseillaise*, the French national anthem. This is surprising. It was composed and sung during the French Revolution by people who executed many aristocrats, including the husband of Jane's own cousin. Another tune she copied and played was *Mr. Handel's Hallelujah Chorus.* This must have sounded very quiet on such a small piano, but there were very few concerts in the country then, and people had to play such music for themselves if they wanted to hear it at all.

If young people wanted to dance, they danced to piano music in their own homes. Mary, the plain sister in *Pride and Prejudice*, played tunes for her sisters to dance to. On 27 December 1808, Jane Austen wrote to her sister:

'Yes, yes, we will have a pianoforte, as good a one as can be got for thirty guineas, and will practise country dances so that we may have some amusement for our nephews and nieces when we have the pleasure of their company'.

◀ Jane Austen's manuscript book and (right)a portrait of her ▶

The Brontës and the piano

The year after Jane Austen died, **Emily Brontë** was born. Emily and her sisters Charlotte and Anne became world-famous novelists. They also learned to play the piano, as before they became successful writers they expected to earn their living as governesses. They learned music by Czerny, Cramer, Bellini, Meyerbeer, and Weber. Emily was a first-class pianist. She studied the piano at the Brussels Conservatoire. Poor Charlotte soon had to stop her lessons as she was too short-sighted to

Emily Brontë ▶

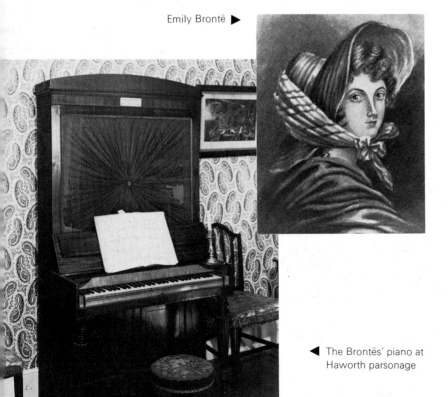

◀ The Brontës' piano at Haworth parsonage

see the music. When she became a governess she could not teach her pupils to play, and had to sew and mend their clothes instead. The Brontë sisters' home, Haworth Parsonage, is now a Museum. There you can see their music books, including Anne's manuscript book of the tunes she enjoyed playing on the piano.

Questions

1 Name some of the different kinds of piano made.
2 Who published a *Pianoforte Magazine*? How many issues did you have to buy to get a free piano?
3 Why did many people learn to play the piano?
4 Can you find the names of five novelists in this chapter?
5 There are the names of six composers in this chapter. Can you find them?
6 What is the French national anthem called? Can you find out why it has this name?

Projects

1 Find out more about Jane Austen, Charlotte, Emily, and Anne Brontë. Make a list of the novels they wrote.
2 A popular dance in the 19th century was the waltz. Can you find the names of other popular dances? Books were published telling people how to perform these dances and the illustrations are often amusing. Look for some pictures and copy one or two.
3 Can you write music as neatly as Jane or Anne? Rule some sets of lines in your book and copy the music in the photograph, or borrow some piano music and copy that instead.
4 Ask a pianist to play the music in the photograph on page 31. Listen and try to follow the music.

Liszt giving a concert in Berlin. His audience seem more interested ▶
in their idol than in listening to the music

6 Rabble-rousers...
or top of the classical pops

The virtuoso

In the 19th century, as towns grew bigger and more prosperous, concert-halls were built. Public piano recitals were given all over Europe. This gave rise to great interest in the **virtuoso** — which means someone who can play an instrument very much better than most. Virtuoso pianists were famous and popular. They earned large sums of money and were the equivalent of the pop-stars of today.

Many famous performers show talent at an early age — often at three, four, or five. Sometimes children who play extraordinarily well do not do so as adults. If they are well taught and practise a great deal they will play well compared with other children. Daily hours of work are needed to keep the fingers and hands supple and to learn new works. If the pianist is not a sensitive musician this will be too demanding. The successful virtuoso needs also an extra gift — a sense of showmanship. But the music must always come first.

All the pianists discussed in this chapter had the qualities needed to become famous. But some seemed to forget the music and present themselves to the audience. In their defence it must be said that some audiences wanted to see their favourite performers rather than to hear them. They talked about the performer rather than about the music. On the other hand some performers won life-long admiration for their respect for the music they played.

Mozart

Of all child prodigies there have ever been, the most gifted was **Wolfgang Amadeus Mozart**. At three he began to play, at five to compose, and at six he gave public concerts. His father taught him and took him on tour. Before he was ten years old Mozart had played in Munich, Vienna, Brussels, Paris, London, Amsterdam, Geneva, and Zurich. He was not an ordinary child. He never went to school, his father taught him all the time, he had no friends of his own age, he practised hard every day. His sister played well, too. Father Leopold Mozart wanted everyone to know how gifted his children were. He liked them to earn money to pay travelling and lodging expenses. He complained in a letter that royal ladies would kiss his children but this didn't pay bills.

The Empress of Austria gave Mozart some Court clothes (everyone wore specially grand clothes to visit royal courts then). There is a picture of Mozart when he was six, wearing the clothes.

◀ A 19th-century concert room in Grosvenor Street, London

▲ The Mozart family. The composer is playing the piano with his sister, Nannerl, while father Leopold looks on

At his concerts the six-year-old Mozart was given newly-written music to sight-read. He also improvised. Sometimes a sheet was held over the keys to hide them and he played just as well as if he could see the keys. He was presented as a wonder-child, a magician rather than as a musician. Audiences wanted to see how clever he was, not to hear music. But when he was grown up the tricks were not so surprising as when he was a child. He still played remarkably well. But he couldn't get a job, and life was hard. His main income came from teaching, from payments from the rich people for whom he composed music, and from giving public concerts. His magnificent piano concertos, which you can listen to, were written to play at these events. You can read more about them on page 39.

Chopin

Chopin was another gifted child. His father arranged for a good musician to teach the boy and only let him give a few concerts for experience. He didn't try to make money out of his son. When Chopin grew up he went to Paris. It was full of talented writers, singers, pianists, and was an exciting place to be. There were many wealthy people who appreciated music. Chopin gave concerts in the homes of the wealthy, in their *salons* (a French word for drawing-room). He gave piano lessons and some (but not many) public concerts. He charged very high fees for both. He was always beautifully dressed, had excellent manners and was always courteous and patient, even with pupils who were slow to see what he wanted. His playing had 'twenty different shades of pianissimo' (very soft playing), as one listener said. He would not play to a chattering audience.

Liszt

Franz Liszt was very different. Accounts of his concerts leave no doubt that he had a very special gift – *charisma* (that means being able to impress other people, influence them, and arouse their admiration. It is like a kind of personal magnetism). Ladies shrieked, fainted, blew kisses, threw flowers at his concerts. People stood up to shout. He would leave his handkerchief on stage and ladies would climb up to grab it, even fight each other for it.

Liszt knew his own worth – and insisted that others know it too. He refused to play for the Queen of Spain because she did not write the invitation herself. He refused to play for the King of Bavaria because they had the same lady-friend. The Czar of

Russia started talking during Liszt's concert – so Liszt stopped playing. He had an enormous number of lovers and two families of children but never married. He was slim, tall, fair, and handsome and he could play faster and louder than anyone else. He had two or even three pianos on stage for one concert as they went out of tune and the strings sometimes broke under his attack. Some critics accused him of thumping but his pupils said he could get a better tone from a piano than anyone else. Other pianists wondered how he could play so accurately when his hands went so high in the air between notes. The composer Mendelssohn, who didn't like him or his playing, still had to admit he was the most musical fast player he (Mendelssohn) had ever heard. No music seemed too difficult for him. He often put in extra notes, more than the composer asked. Chopin hated anyone messing about with his music like this and told Liszt so, but it made no difference. Liszt treated him like everyone else.

Clara Schumann

Clara Schumann (1819–1896) was born Clara Wieck. Until she was three she was slow to speak or understand speech. Her father didn't seem to like her. One day he heard her making harmonious sounds on the piano. She made sense of the piano although she could speak very little. Father Wieck thought he might have a child prodigy in his daughter and began intensive training. Her mother couldn't stand it and left the home.

Clara talked of her childhood in later life. She was not allowed to read books. She had to practise scales and exercises. Her father tore up the music she enjoyed if her playing did not please him. When she was 16 she was said to be the best pianist in Europe.

Robert and Clara Schumann ▶

Trouble came when **Robert Schumann** (see page 41) wanted to marry her. Her father forbade the marriage but she rebelled and did marry. They had eight children and she kept up her practising although she gave very few concerts. When she was 35 her husband's death left her to support the children alone. She gave many concerts then and taught pupils for the rest of her life. She was not a showy pianist like Liszt. She said some very unkind things about his style of playing, in fact, thinking it was too noisy. She played a lot of Beethoven's music when it was not considered popular. She was the first musician to play in public without music. Now all pianists do, but she was the first. When she grew older and her memory was less good, she sat on the music to help her remember it.

Paderewski

Ignacy Jan Paderewski (1860–1941) was the first concert pianist to tour America using a private train and taking with him his piano-tuner, hairdresser, chef, butler, and wife. He gave concerts as a child, but was mostly self-taught and developed a lot of technical faults. Although he had lessons from a good teacher when he was older, his bad habits stayed with him and he was always uncertain in performance. He was always nervous when performing, and he gave too many concerts too quickly, before he had built up a repertory. Fellow-musicians criticized his playing. The playwright and music-critic George Bernard Shaw called him a 'spirited harmonious blacksmith'. Some recordings of his playing, made in 1909, seem to show that his critics were right. But, as Harold Schonberg says in *The Great Pianists,* 'while his competitors were counting his wrong notes, he was counting his dollars'. This was because he had golden curly hair, which attracted the ladies, and plenty of newspaper publicity. Audiences went wild with excitement when he played, and he was besieged by autograph hunters. He bought a castle in Spain with his first earnings, and became Prime Minister of Poland after the First World War.

Cartoon of Paderewski playing the piano ▲

Questions

1 How differently did Mozart's father and Chopin's father treat their sons?
2 What does *charisma* mean?
3 How did Liszt play the piano?
4 Who was the first pianist to play in public without music? What happened when the pianist's memory began to fail?
5 Who was the first pianist to tour America in his own train?

Projects

1 Use reference books to discover more about the pianists mentioned in this book. Try to find out about other gifted children. Chess-players often show talent at an early age. Collect all the information you can on one or two.
2 Make a time-table of how you spend your week. Could you fit into it several hours practising every day? What would you give up, or stop doing to make time for the practice? Would it be worth it, to be famous?

7 Music for the piano

GRANDE
SONATE

Grave

Grande Sonate pathétique
Pour le Clavecin ou Piano Forte
Composée et dediée
À Son Altesse Monseigneur le Prince
CHARLES DE LICHNOWSKY
par
Louis Van Beethoven
Oeuvre 13. N.º 56

A Vienne chez Hoffmeister.

When pianos were first made publishers began to print 'Music for Keyboard'. They hoped to sell it to people both with harpsichords *and* pianos. But it was soon realized, first by Clementi, that piano music should exploit (make the most of) the piano's special characteristics.

The sonata and concerto

The two most important types of piano music from about 1780 onwards were the **sonata** and the **concerto**. A sonata was a piece for piano alone. It usually had four movements:

a A lively first movement, with two or three contrasting tunes (or themes)

b A slow movement with song-like tunes

c A minuet – a stately dance in three-time

d A quick and lively fast movement, often with a gay tune that came several times over. This was called a **rondo**.

Not all piano sonatas followed this pattern. Some had only three movements instead of four. Later composers, such as Liszt, even wrote very long sonatas all in one movement. Beethoven's 'Moonlight' Sonata begins with a slow movement instead of a fast one. Some sonatas had a set of variations instead of a rondo as the last movement. A short, simple sonata for young players was called a **sonatina**. Clementi wrote some of these. (See page 22.)

Haydn (1732–1809) and Mozart (1756–1791) wrote sonatas for harpsichord and later for the piano. Beethoven (1770–1827) wrote 32 sonatas for piano. And he always seemed to be ahead of the piano-makers. His sonatas used a wider and wider range of notes as more were added to the piano keyboard.

◀ The first edition of Beethoven's *Pathétique* sonata, printed in 1800; the opening of the sonata and (inset) the title page

Beethoven's sonatas are very varied. There are song-like tunes with rich, low, chord accompaniments. The gay tunes in the last movements skip and dance and leap across the keys. You discover something new every time you listen to them. (They are not easy to play and were not thought easy to listen to for over a hundred years after they were written.)

A **concerto** was a piece for solo piano with orchestral accompaniment. It usually had three movements – like the sonata but without the minuet. Near the end of the first movement there was often a cadenza – a section not written down by the composer, but made up (improvised) by the pianist as he went along. Pianists were expected to dazzle their audiences in a cadenza by a display of technical virtuosity.

Mozart wrote 27 piano concertos. They are the most perfect things he ever wrote for the piano. Some of them, such as those in G major (K.453), and A major (K.488) are lively and sparkling. Others, such as the D minor (K.466) and C minor (K.491) are powerful and even tragic in mood. They were written for Mozart himself to play, and perhaps through them, more than anything else he wrote, Mozart was able to express his own joys and sorrows.

Beethoven wrote five fine piano concertos. The fifth is known as the 'Emperor'. They are all written on a bigger scale than Mozart's – so Beethoven took up where Mozart left off.

The piano concerto continued to be popular throughout the 19th century. However, where Mozart had written 27, and Beethoven five, later composers tended only to write one or two. The most famous of these are the ones by Schumann, Grieg, Brahms (two), and Tchaikovsky. Rakhmaninov (1873–1943) wrote four, of which the second is the most popular. In all these later concertos, the orchestra gradually became more and more prominent, so that instead of just accompanying the piano, it took up a position of equal importance. In many of these works, the soloist almost seems to be fighting with the orchestra.

Schubert and the piano

When Beethoven was dying, a young composer in Vienna was writing in a new way for the piano. **Franz Schubert** (1797–1828) trained as a choir-boy in the Cathedral in Vienna. He began writing symphonies and songs while still at school. He became the most famous and prolific (that means productive) song-writer there has ever been. When Schubert died he left over 600 songs. The special thing about his songs was the way the piano part created the right atmosphere for the singer. The tunes are very singable and stick in your head long after you hear them. *Serenade, Hark, Hark, the Lark, The Trout,* and *The Hedge-rose* are some of the most often sung.

One of Schubert's most exciting songs is a setting of a poem by Goethe – *The Erl-King*. This describes a father riding home on horseback through a forest at night. He rides fast as his son, whom he holds in his arms, is ill. The father rides faster, and at last reaches home. The boy is dead in his arms.

The piano part of *The Erl-King* is one of the most difficult ever written. Schubert said it made his wrist ache when he played it. A non-stop galloping triplet (three-note) figure in the left hand imitates the horse's hooves. Harsh chords clash with the singer's notes when the boy cries out. There is a catchy, swoopy tune when the Erl-King, who is death, tries to tempt the boy to come with him. The piano is silent when the father reaches home and the voice alone sings that the boy is dead.

Schubert's piano solos are very tuneful. As well as sonatas and long works, he wrote some *Impromptus*. This means 'made up on the spur of the moment'. They were a new kind of composition. There are eight – two sets of four. Each set makes a complete whole, rather like a sonata.

▲ Franz Schubert

▲ Felix Mendelssohn

▲ An illustration for *The Erl-King*

Mendelssohn, Schumann and Chopin

Felix Mendelssohn (1809–1847) was the son of a very rich man. This meant that he had a good general and musical education as well as every opportunity to devote his time and energy to music. Yet he died young, from overwork, and his composing suffered from his doing too many other things. He conducted, played the piano, organized music festivals, encouraged other composers, toured Europe, visited England. He played to Queen Victoria and her husband, Prince Albert, who liked him and his music. His piano pieces called *Songs without Words* are full of variety and fairly easy to play. Some clever pianists despised them because they were easy, but they were very popular with ordinary pianists.

Robert Schumann (1810–1856) wrote pieces for his eight children when they were learning to play the piano. *Album for the Young* is still enjoyed by young pianists and so is *Scenes from Childhood.* If you can't play them yourself, try to get a friend to play some of them for you, or listen to a record.

The Polish composer **Frédéric Chopin** (1810–1849) wrote for the piano in a new, revolutionary way. No one had ever before used the piano as he did. He combined strange, discordant harmony with delicate, decorated melodies that are so singable

that lots of his tunes were borrowed to make pop-tunes in the 1940s and 1950s. He wrote stormy and thunderous *Polonaises.* The polonaise was a dance but Chopin used the rhythm of the dance to represent the Polish cavalry. Russia had conquered Poland then and many Polish people, like Chopin, went to live abroad.

Chopin wrote four sonatas that were very different from those of Mozart and Beethoven. One sonata is called the *Funeral March Sonata.* The slow movement is a Funeral March with a lovely slow tune in the middle section. He also wrote **waltzes** — to be listened to, not for dancing — **nocturnes**, **preludes**, **ballades**, **scherzos** and 24 **studies**.

The studies, or *études* (the French word Chopin used) are splendid to hear. Each gives exercise in a technical problem such as broken chords (chords played one note at a time very fast), arpeggios (chords played one note at a time running from top to bottom or bottom to top of the keyboard), rapidly-repeated notes, rapidly-repeated chords, scale-passages, chromatic passages (using every note on the piano, black and white) and leaping octaves (played with thumb and little finger together). They are fun to listen to. Many have nicknames that listeners like to use although Chopin wouldn't have used them. Opus 10 means the composer's tenth work to be published. Number 5 means the fifth piece in that book. Chopin's study Opus 10 No. 5 is called the 'Black Key'. Opus 10 No. 12 is called the 'Revolutionary'. (He wrote it when he heard the Russians had invaded Poland.) Opus 25 No. 1 is 'The Aeolian Harp'. Opus 25 No. 11 is 'The Winter Wind'.

▼ Polonaise in A major, opus 40 no. 1, by Chopin

Some later composers for the piano

Liszt's music always sounds very difficult. It is. If Liszt found that other people could play his works, he made them even harder when he himself played them again, by putting in more notes. He wrote many **transcriptions**. These are decorated arrangements for piano of orchestral works, operas, and songs.

Brahms's works are difficult but not showy, like those of Liszt. As well as sonatas, he wrote short pieces – **intermezzos**, **rhapsodies**, **capriccios** and **waltzes**.

Debussy (1862–1918) was a Frenchman and his music was different altogether from that of Brahms or Liszt. If you look at paintings by the French Impressionists (a name they got because of the way they painted – trying to give the 'impression' of a subject by little dots and smudges of colour), you will *see* the kind of thing you *hear* in Debussy's music. If that sounds odd, try it, and you will discover what it means.

Some of Debussy's music describes things you wouldn't expect a piano to be able to describe – 'Fountains', 'Goldfish', 'Footsteps in the Snow' and 'The Submerged Cathedral'. Debussy made unusual use of the pedal and of the **sympathetic vibration** which you discovered on page 13. People had just got used to Chopin's unusual harmonies when Debussy introduced even more unusual ones.

Satie (1866–1925) was a friend of Debussy. He was laughed at when he wrote his music, but really he asked for it. He wrote odd remarks on his music. One set of five pieces was called 'Three Pieces in the Shape of a Pear', and sounded so odd that people didn't know what to make of them. You may know his piece called *Gymnopédie*. What the title means is anybody's guess. Another set of pieces is called 'Flabby Preludes (for a Dog)'. His expression marks are different from anyone else's too. Players are told to play 'with a wink' and 'with surprise' and to 'open your head'.

Questions

1 Who wrote 27 piano concertos?
2 Who wrote 32 piano sonatas?
3 Who is the Erl-King? What happens to the boy?
4 What does the piano imitate in the song about the 'Erl-King'?
5 What part of the piano did Debussy make special use of?

Projects

1 Listen to the two different performances of a Schubert song (choose a song you can get two recordings of, but try to hear the 'Erl-King'). Compare the performances, say how they are different and which you prefer and why.
2 Listen to some Chopin studies – those with titles or nick-names are popular. Which do you like best? Can you say why?
3 Collect some postcards or pictures of Impressionist paintings by Monet, Manet, Degas, Renoir, Pissarro, Sisley, Cézanne. Look at them and try to describe them. Listen to some music by Debussy. Try to describe what you hear.

The jazz pianist Oscar Peterson and the conductor André Previn, who is also a jazz pianist ▶

8 The 20th century

It is much easier to play records, cassettes, and radio than it is to play the piano and there are far fewer piano-pupils now than there were a hundred years ago. But there are some extraordinarily gifted young performers, more, probably, than there have ever been. Concerts are heard more on TV and radio, although there are less in local concert-halls. Travelling today is faster and easier than it was and there are many **international piano competitions**.

At these a panel of judges is chosen. They listen as young performers play many difficult pieces. The best players are chosen to play a piano concerto with an orchestra. The winners get money-prizes, contracts to play concerts all over the world, and some go on to become world-famous. These competitions happen in places like Warsaw, Texas, Moscow, Leeds, Budapest, usually every three or four years. Past winners include famous pianists like John Lill, John Ogden, Radu Lupu, David Wilde, Michel Dalberto, Van Cliburn, and Murray Perahia.

▲ The Russian composer Shostakovich presenting a gold medal to the American pianist Van Cliburn at the first Tchaikovsky International Competition in Moscow (1958).

Some modern composers for the piano

Composers have used the piano in new ways. Players are occasionally directed to leave the keys and sound the strings by touching them directly with their fingers.

Ives

Charles Ives (1874–1954) was an American, brought up in Danbury, Connecticut, where his father ran the town band and gave music lessons. Charles experimented with sounds from an early age. He wanted to write music his own way, without worrying about whether it was popular and whether it was earning him money. So he earned money (a lot of it) in business and wrote just the kind of music he liked. It is just becoming popular now, a long time after his death. He stopped writing when he wished to, which was many years before he died.

In a piano piece called *Majority* (1915) the player is asked to use the forearm to sound ten neighbouring black notes at once, and to hold them down while the left hand plays chords and a melody. Then the left forearm is asked to sound 14 neighbouring white notes at once and hold them while the right hand plays normally. Ives's *Concord Sonata* is one of the most difficult pieces of piano music ever written. Each of its movements is named after a famous person or persons who lived in the town of Concord, Massachusetts. One of the movements is the 'Alcotts' (the family which included Louisa Alcott, who wrote *Little Women*).

Like Bartók (see page 45) Ives used folk-tunes. He also used popular hymn-tunes such as 'Nearer my God to Thee' as well as 'Turkey in the Straw' and 'Campdown Races'. Also like Bartók, he used irregular rhythms. In his first piano sonata the left hand has *two* quavers while the right hand plays *ten* semiquavers, for four bars. Then, suddenly, the left hand has to fit *seven* quavers under the ten semiquavers. In the next bar the right hand has to fit in extra semiquavers to the left hand's four quavers. As the names tell you, a semiquaver is half as long as a quaver.

Rakhmaninov

Sergey Rakhmaninov (1873–1943) was a world-famous concert pianist as well as a composer. His best-known works are four piano concertos, *Rhapsody on a Theme of Paganini* for piano and orchestra (very enjoyable to listen to), and many sets of solo piano pieces, especially *Preludes* and *Études-Tableaux* ('Study-Pictures').

Ravel

Maurice Ravel (1875–1937) is famous for colourful, brilliantly-scored orchestral music (*Bolero, La Valse, Rhapsodie Espagnole*). He wrote much piano music, in a style partly like Debussy (see page 42), partly using spiky harmonies and rhythms all his own. *Le Tombeau de Couperin* ('In Memory of Couperin') and *Gaspard de la Nuit* ('Gaspard of the Night') are two of his best works for solo piano. You may hear his two piano concertos, too (the second is for left-hand alone), and his most famous piece of all, *Pavane pour une infante défunte* ('Dance for a Dead Princess') — a piece which became so popular that he detested it, because no one seemed interested in his other music.

Prokofiev

Sergey Prokofiev (1891–1953) is best known for his *Classical Symphony* and *Peter and the Wolf.* He wrote much piano music: five concertos (listen first to No. 3), nine sonatas, and collections of shorter works with titles like *Sarcasms, Fleeting Visions, Stories of an Old Grandmother.*

▲ A cartoonist's impression of the Hungarian composer, Béla Bartók

Bartók

Béla Bartók (1881–1945) was a pianist, a child prodigy. He was born on the border of Romania and Hungary. He collected folk songs from these areas and from Bulgaria, and this music excited him and has a strong influence on his compositions. Debussy (see page 42) had also felt excited by Eastern music when he heard it and he used the *pentatonic* scale in his piano music. (Play the black notes in turn and you will get the idea of that scale.) The folk music of Bartók's part of Eastern Europe

45

had strong, irregular rhythms which did not divide into bars of equal length. Bartók, using these kind of rhythms, used very odd time-signatures such as

$$\frac{4+2+3}{8}$$

and

$$\frac{2+2+3}{8}$$

to contain the rhythms.

He composed a set of pieces called *Mikrokosmos* (meaning 'small world') from 1926 onwards, beginning with easy pieces for beginners and ending with difficult pieces for concert pianists. Other famous works include a sonata, three concertos and a clangy piece called *Allegro barbaro*.

Messaien

Oliver Messiaen (born in France, 1908) wrote a book explaining the way he built his music. The book is called *Modes de valeurs et d'intensités.* He describes twelve ways of playing one note, seven degrees of loudness, twenty-four rhythms, as well as using pitch in the usual way. His work is very difficult to play and his wife, Yvonne Loriod, is a brilliant pianist. He himself is a church organist, has written a great deal of religious music, and is very interested in birdsong. His piece for the piano and orchestra called *Oiseaux exotiques* is unusual in that every note is a birdsong theme. His 90-minute-long *Vingt Regards sur L'Enfant Jésus* ('20 Looks at the Child Jesus'), and the equally long *Catalogue d'Oiseaux* ('Bird Catalogue'), based on birdsong, are fascinating, exciting works.

Cage

John Cage (born in America, 1912) like Satie (see page 42) is interested in a new approach to sound and to the part the performer plays. His teacher Schoenberg said Cage was not a composer, but an inventor of genius. Cage's most unusual piece of piano music is entitled *4' 33"* because it lasts for 4 minutes and 33 seconds. The pianist walks to the piano with his music and sits there but his page of music is blank. Nothing is played. Any sounds that happen inside or outside the concert-hall become the music.

Piano Concert has 33 pages of music containing sounds that can be played in any order. The performer decides whether all of it, or just some of it, happens. The pianist may have an orchestra if he or she wishes. The orchestra may be large or small, may play all or some of its music. As you can guess, every performance is different!

The composer John Cage ▶

▲ A prepared piano

Uses of the piano today

The piano is sometimes used as an ordinary member of the modern symphony orchestra. In this case the piano is not put in the centre (as it is when playing the solo in a piano concerto) but is put near the drums in the percussion section.

The piano is still a useful leader of the music if your school performs a musical or an opera. It keeps everyone together as the harpsichordist used to do in the 18th century.

The piano is used instead of a full orchestra by ballet-dancers and opera-singers when they are rehearsing. It can cover as many notes as a full orchestra. (It is also cheaper to pay one pianist than a full orchestra, and easier to stop and start when practising difficult parts over and over again.) The pianist who plays in opera rehearsals is called a *répétiteur* (French for 'repeater').

Cage also 'prepares' pianos by placing rubber, plastic, screws and bolts at certain measured points between the strings. This alters the tone quality. *Sonatas and Interludes* (1946–8) uses a **prepared piano**; it is a beautiful tinkling piece, with a partly Indian or Far Eastern sound (Eastern music uses 'chance' in the same sort of way as Cage).

Cage thus introduces two special interests – sounds in themselves, that is not joined to make chords or tunes; and how the performer can contribute by deciding what sounds to use and which to ignore.

Several young British composers are excited by what Cage has done, including **Bill Hopkins**, **Anthony Paine**, **Giles Swayne**, and **Brian Chapple**, who had a great success with his composition for four pianos called *Cantos* at the 1978 Promenade Concerts.

Two famous pianists of today, John Ogdon (left) and Vladimir Ashkenazy ▶

The piano in jazz

Jazz is a long subject for the space we have left, and it is the subject of many specialist books which you will find in your local libraries. It uses the piano as a solo instrument as well as with groups of jazz musicians. The piano is important in these groups because it can play chords and keep the all-important chord-sequence (the framework of the other players' improvisations) going. You can hear on TV or records fine jazz pianists like **Art Tatum, Oscar Peterson,** or **Dave Brubeck.**

▲ The piano in big band: Count Basie

▲ And in pop: Elton John

Questions

1 Which pianists play jazz? How many more can you discover who are not mentioned in this book?
2 What new uses have modern composers made of the piano?

Projects

1 Collect information about, and pictures of, a performer or composer who interests you. Perhaps you can give a talk to your class about your chosen musician, and illustrate it by means of records or tapes.
2 Look through record catalogues. How many records are issued of piano works? Is this less or more than the records made of other instruments? Which pianists are most popular (i.e. have the largest number of records on sale)?

◄ The jazz pianist and composer Dave Brubeck

(*inside back cover*) Jelly Roll Morton and his band, the Red Hot Peppers, in the 1920s